infant

INSPIRATION

Cheers to your
amazing journey
as a Mom!

XO,
Amy

An Enlightening Perspective on How Newborns
Teach Mothers Essential Life Lessons

infant

INSPIRATION

insights
that encourage
serenity & awe

by Amy Collins
Illustrated by Jessica Wu

iUniverse

INFANT INSPIRATION
AN ENLIGHTENING PERSPECTIVE ON HOW NEWBORNS TEACH MOTHERS ESSENTIAL LIFE LESSONS

iUniverse books may be ordered through booksellers or by contacting:

iUniverse
1663 Liberty Drive
Bloomington, IN 47403
www.iuniverse.com
1-800-Authors (1-800-288-4677)

ISBN: 978-1-5320-6547-7 (sc)
ISBN: 978-1-5320-6549-1 (hc)
ISBN: 978-1-5320-6548-4 (e)

Library of Congress Control Number: 2018912876

Print information available on the last page.

iUniverse rev. date: 01/21/2019

Contents

Acknowledgements

Thank you, Kathryn and Courtney, for continually teaching me. It's a fascinating process to evolve together daily. It's messy at times, but overall absolutely amazing.

I've learned that life is about the choices we make and how our choices create who we are and our lifestyle. My hope is that you continue to make healthy choices that align with who you are at your core. I'm thankful because my role as your mom has truly strengthened my faith. I pray daily for guidance to help nurture you to become the best versions of you. As I say, "Learning every day is what keeps life interesting." So let's keep learning together throughout our journey!

I love being with both of you, and just when I think I love you as much as possible, I love you even more. It sounds crazy, I know, but I never understood a mother's love until I became one. And it's truly indescribable.

Thank you for being dynamic young women. I pray you continue to shine your light and cherish life's simple blessings. God bless you, my chicks.

Of course, thank you also to my wonderful husband for his continual support. Raising children continues to teach us more than we could have ever imagined. I'm glad we're on this ride of a lifetime *together*! Let's keep learning *and* laughing - I love you, Pat.

"Never leave a true relation for a few faults. Nobody is perfect. Nobody is correct at the end. Affection is always greater than perfection."
                    Buddha's Teaching & Science

Introduction

As a mom, it's normal to feel like you need to teach your baby everything, but have you ever thought about what you can learn from your baby? Our infants can also teach us several valuable life lessons. By cultivating this perspective, as well as the traditional one of moms teaching babies, an even stronger and more joyful mother/child foundation is established. A solid starting point, will better enable both of you to be your best selves. Additionally, this insight encourages your faith to flourish.

I want to take a moment, dear reader, and assure you that I'm aware of how the word *God* connotes different ideas for each of us; therefore, although the word *God* works best for me, please choose whatever word works best for you. There are many ways to express our faith, and my personal belief is that every sense of spirituality that believes in goodness ultimately leads to the same greater source. As you will read, for me, it's my personal connection with a loving and faithful God; however, I want you to honor whatever works best for you.

This book's intention is to make a positive and personal impact to help you as Mom feel more peaceful, build a solid foundation in your relationship with your child so you both thrive, and deepen your faith.

"All religions, arts and sciences are branches of the same tree."
Albert Einstein

"The essence of all religions is one. Only their approaches are different."
Mahatma Gandhi

Welcome

Congratulations on your newborn! Your journey of motherhood promises to be like no other adventure you've ever experienced. Hopefully these lessons will enable you to build a strong foundation for your mother/child relationship to flourish as well as strengthen your faith.

After I gave birth to my daughters, I was in awe of them and truly believed they were each a gift. However, as a new mother (and even to this day), it became clear to me that God keeps sending us babies to teach, or at least remind, us of some very basic yet essential life lessons. If we take the time to notice these lessons and put them into practice (not only during the first few months but also the years to come), they help us cultivate a close relationship with each other and God.

As a result, these lessons led me to develop an overall sense of peace, joy, and love. As a mom, I continue to recognize that having these core attributes is essential because, when we are able to lean on them, they empower us to stay grounded as we bump up against the craziness in our world and help our children navigate through it.

When my daughters were both infants, I journaled what I was learning from them. These pages contain the various lessons I learned. Each lesson helped me shape my relationship with my children; I grew stronger in my faith and became more peaceful.

To this day, when I am able to call a lesson into action, a feeling of peace transpires. This feeling leads to joy, joy to love, and love back to peace. It's a circular energy that, when put into motion, enables us to live with a sense of grounded-ness and security. My hope is that, as we consciously choose to put these lessons into practice, we create an intrinsically uplifting sensation one person at a time and peace spreads.

In just the first months of my daughters' lives—without them even knowing it—they reminded me of these fundamental aspects of life and helped me put them into practice. So in the midst of changing diapers and in between feedings and naps, my advice is to be mindful of your time with your baby, listen to your child, watch him or her, be present with him or her, enjoy this stage, and learn together as you lay the groundwork of your relationship. My own thought is that God is speaking to us through our precious infants. We need to be mindful enough to listen and learn from them.

So take some deep breaths and remember that this infant phase shall pass. My mom still says, "Some days may seem long, but the years go by quickly." And they do! I encourage you to enjoy your newborn. Hopefully a beautiful outcome of this stage will be that the lessons your infant teaches you, you teach your baby, and the ones you learn together will create a solid sense of trust, peace, joy, and love that will serve as the cornerstones of your mother/child relationship. Hopefully, your faith will also flourish and you will live more peacefully.

May you learn daily as your journey of motherhood continues on in ways that will amaze you. My hope is that these lessons serve to help you build a meaningful, authentic and lasting bond with your child and your God. Peace be with you.

At the time Jesus said, "I praise You, Father, Lord of heaven and earth, that You have hidden these things from the wise and intelligent and have revealed them to infants."
Matthew 11:25 (NASB)

Lesson 1

we are not alone

I remember the first night we brought home our oldest daughter. We tucked her into her bassinet, and she fell sound asleep. My husband and I took a couple of deep sighs and cozied up, ready for a much-needed night sleep. All of a sudden, we heard this ever so quiet, but very distinct, little sneeze. Yep, that was our baby!

That sneeze surprised us in such a surreal and funny way that we both just started laughing. It was as if she were saying, "I'm here too!" She was reminding us that we were not alone. That is true. Once you are a mother, you are not alone. As we welcome our babies, they become part of us like another appendage and then eventually grow to become our little tagalongs, sidekicks, teens, and someday hopefully one of our closest adult friends.

Our children remind us that we are all God's children, He is always with us, and we need Him the way our children need us. Once we become moms, we are exposed to a depth of love that we have never experienced before. We instinctively realize our children need us in a way that no one has ever needed us before.

Hence, God reminds us that we need Him in this same way. God is always by our side, guiding, nurturing, healing, and unconditionally loving us. As we begin this journey of motherhood by also guiding, nurturing, healing, and unconditionally loving our babies, let us remember God is with us. Through the simple presence of our children, God reminds us first and foremost that we are always His children and therefore we are never alone.

Have I not commanded you? Be strong and courageous.
Do not be afraid; do not be discouraged, for the LORD
your God will be with you wherever you go.
Joshua 1:9 (NIV)

Lesson 2

pause & listen

Oftentimes when we are in a conversation, we know what we want to say next, and sometimes we are so excited to express our thoughts that we interrupt the other person. Sound familiar? Our babies remind us that it is important to completely listen to the other person because, when we listen, we learn. The other person has the ability to share a different perspective or new idea with us, which encourages us to grow. Even though our infants can't express themselves in words, we still need to pause and listen to them. Once we listen, then we can determine how to best help them.

On the flip side, let's remember that our babies are also listening carefully to us and are learning what our different vocal tonalities mean and how we converse with other people. They are listening to how a conversation flows. Are we exemplifying ebb-and-flow conversations? I remember when my chicks would coo; I would coo back and then listen and wait for them to respond. This simple game teaches them the very basics of conversational flow. Listening is a key part of any *true* conversation.

With God, we often rush in and tell Him what we want as well as how and when we want it. Come on. Fess up - we all do it! But we need to remember to pause and listen to God. He speaks to us through loved ones, strangers, animals, written passages, nature, and even loss. God is constantly finding ways to have us listen to Him. With enough persistence through either subtle or loud action, God hopes His will gets through to us. What is our prayer time like? Are we listening or constantly pushing for our own desires? How often do we look to pause and listen?

It is amazing how, once we begin listening, we learn so much about each other, ourselves, our purpose and our world. As soon as we listen, we see vivid messages guiding us in various ways. Although listening in our current world is underrated, it is essential to create authentic relationships. So let's embrace the art of listening and install it as a cornerstone as we build the foundation of our mother/child relationship and our relationship with God, too.

My dear brothers and sisters, take note of this: Everyone should be quick to listen, slow to speak and slow to become angry.

James 1:19 (NIV)

Lesson 3

let's slow down

No matter who we are, we all have twenty-four hours in a day, and as we logically know, that doesn't change when we have a newborn. Time with those we love is a tremendous gift. Therefore, making time to spend with this new family member is especially important to create a genuine relationship.

We can enjoy lively activities with our babies or simply read next to each other in the same room, yet the most valuable time together is when we are truly present with one another. Let's face it - our world today is rigged to distract us. When a baby comes into our world, we have a choice. We can either try to maintain our previous lifestyle or make adjustments, which often entails slowing down. I coined the term *life maintenance* to refer to all of that stuff we need to do to stay on course.

Once we bring home our infant, we need to take intentional breaks, disconnect from the doing and truly connect with each other. We can't put off doing the dishes, paying the bills, washing the laundry, or going to our jobs forever, but we can become more aware of when we take care of this life maintenance and our attitude about how it fits in with our new role as Mom.

When we consciously choose to slow down, an unparalleled sense of calmness ensues and this enable us to more fully enjoy our newborn. Since our infants need so much of our time and attention to satisfy even their most basic needs, we just don't have as much time to do everything else we used to do. Due to our new role as Mom, we need to be aware that it is also acceptable to have a changed attitude towards all that life maintenance. We want to make the time to develop a relationship with our new little loved one since time with our child is our greatest gift. We never know how long this opportunity will last. Realistically - babies grow up and people die - we have no guarantees, so let's slow down and connect.

The same is true with our need to slow down and make time to be with God and notice His presence in our world. When we slow down with our babies, it's an ideal time to also develop a close relationship with God. During those quiet late-night feedings, instead of getting frustrated, pray. Think of all those other parents who are also up with their newborns and pray for them too. Share with God both the joy and exhaustion you are feeling. Either way, He wants you to spend time with Him. Learn to see the face of God in your infant and know that God loves you as much as you love your new baby.

God and your baby deserve your time. Delight in being present with them. Slowing down doesn't mean constantly texting or scrolling through Pinterest with your baby next to you or that as you watch TV, you are also being with God. Slow down enough to be truly present with each other and get to know each other without any distractions. When you are genuinely still and focus on each other, you will both feel a sense of peace. After all, let's remember our relationships with loved ones are what matter most in life, not all that other *life maintenance.*

"Do not run until your feet are bare and your throat is dry."
Jeremiah 2:25 (NIV)

Lesson 4

choose trust

Do you think we are born knowing fear, or do we learn fear from the world around us? Besides instinctual fear, which helps us survive, I think other fears are mostly learned. Therefore, I see our newborns as symbols of faith and trust. Each day brings new challenges as they learn new things like how to eat, sit, and roll. All of this learning takes trust. Therefore, we need to teach our children to trust and live courageously. Learn caution, yes, but not fear. As we raise them with this mindset, we encourage continual learning of new ideas about everything such as different cultures, religions, and countries.

Despite knowing we can trust God, we learn fear. But God does not want us to live in fear, just like we don't want this for our children. God does *not* want us to give in to all this manipulated worldly fear. He wants us to be courageous and trust enough to share our gifts and make a positive impact on our world. He wants us to trust while simultaneously being proactive.

God created us to enjoy life, not live in fear of it. He created us to be able to see beauty, touch each other, smell flowers, taste homemade cookies, hear music, laugh, and, above all, use the talents we've been given to express love. If we live in fear of what others think or of what might happen, then we never allow our own light to fully shine. Our newborns are who they are; they simply are born to shine fearlessly. So, let's choose also to embody trust and encourage our children's natural trust so we can all shine as we are meant to do.

Trust lays the foundation for peace. Babies are born 100 percent dependent; therefore, they have no choice but to trust us completely to take care of, protect, guide, and love them. As we grow up, we learn how to do many activities on our own, but we need to remember that ultimately we need to trust each other in order to help each other. Even though loss and pain are part of life, we can choose to keep trusting. Our babies exemplify this sense of trust, which enables them to be peaceful. Doesn't that sound wonderful - to be peaceful?

However, as many of us become more independent, we also often become more stressed because we think we need to do it all on our own. We forget to trust God to help and guide us. When we combine proactivity with a true sense of trust, God shows us the way. Instead of developing the mindset that we are completely independent, we must remember that, like our babies who instinctively are born to trust us, we are and always will be God's children so we need to trust Him. Let's continue to be proactive in our lives, yet know that when we also put our trust in God, we are much more peaceful.

You will keep in perfect peace those whose minds are steadfast because they trust in you.
Isaiah 26:3 (NIV)

Lesson 5

encouraging a playful spirit

Sometimes we hear people say, "Oh, to be young again!" as they sigh and those around them share reminiscent looks. Although we may not be physically young, our spirit can remain youthful. After all, we are forever God's children. If we let ourselves, we can still act as silly as a one-, five-, ten-, or sixteen-year-old. Playing is possible at any age! We have a fun opportunity to view our babies as the perfect excuse to play! Our children love when we share in their imaginative world of play. Yet we can also play with our spouse, siblings, parents, and friends no matter what our age. It is necessary to accept and respect how our physical capabilities change, but we can still maintain a playful spirit.

The Bible encourages us to enjoy life. Jesus enjoyed His friends and must have been quite charismatic and even playful to attract so many followers. If we open up to how God works a sense of playfulness into our lives, then maybe we won't become overly serious as we grow older. God wants us to remain joyful like our babies and maintaining a playful spirit enables us to do just that - stay joyful.

Does this mean we will never have problems? No. Does this mean we will not have to work? No. Children are born with a natural desire to imagine and explore their environments through play; as adults, we need to maintain our sense of imagination and exploration. Let's be playful role models so we bolster our children's natural desires to play - in an unstructured creative way. Maintaining and encouraging a playful spirit results in a more joyful world which is better for all of us.

The city streets will be filled with boys and girls playing there.
Zechariah 8:5 (NIV)

Lesson 6

share your smile

A smile is such an easy gesture to extend to other people, and most of the time, babies do it instinctively and frequently. That is how we should all smile—naturally and often. After all, smiling takes barely any effort, only entails a few seconds of our time, and is a completely free gift to share with anyone you want.

Smiling at everyone is really fun because of how different people react, for example, a quick smile back, a perplexed look that reads "What is she so happy about?" or a broad, genuine grin. It's entertaining to see people's reactions!

Another response is sometimes one of thankfulness because, when we look at people and smile, we recognize them, and we all have an innate need to be recognized. The hope is that, when someone smiles back at me, the ripple effect will be set in motion. As that person continues on, he or she will smile at someone else. And on and on it goes. The idea is that smiles will become more readily exchanged and more plentiful, making our world a more cheerful place one person at a time.

It was interesting how so many people smiled at me when I was with my newborn. They'd look at my baby and smile at her, and then when I looked at them, they'd smile at me too. Even if our babies are a bit more serious, they inevitably provoke smiles from others just because they are amazing little miracles. Isn't it ironic that babies cause so many people to smile, yet as we grow up, we sometimes hesitate before we smile? God gave us this ability to smile in order to create a strong sense of connectedness.

Nowadays, whenever my girls ask me if they look okay, I respond, "Sure - but what's your best accessory?" And they beam and say, "Our smile." Let's use this simple ability to recognize each other and develop more truly engaging communities.

A cheerful look brings joy to the heart;
good news makes for good health.
Proverbs 15:30 (NASB)

Lesson 7

sweet affection

It's been proven that affection helps babies grow stronger and improves their mental development. But it doesn't help only infants. Although let's admit it, our babies are just so darn easy to smooch! They remind us, just by being themselves, how essential sweet affection is to our well-being. We all need affection, no matter what age we are. Various studies also show evidence that, when someone is appropriately and sensitively touched by another, he or she feels more at ease.

Our sense of touch is precious, and we need to extend simple, appropriate gestures to each other—like hugs, hand holding, a pat on the back or a reaching out of a kind hand—any one of these gestures can help someone. To some people, being affectionate comes naturally, while others sometimes learn how to become more demonstrative. Either way, the guarantee is that, once you begin the motion of extending genuine, supportive affection, you will help others, and oftentimes it comes right back around and helps us too.

Our bodies are given to us to be orchestrated as tools to communicate with and help lift and strengthen others. God reminds us to use our bodies in this gentle way to help us sense His presence. Let's remember that our ability to extend sweet affection is a simple way to do that.

> *Love each other with genuine affection, and*
> *take delight in honoring each other.*
> Romans 12:10 (NLT)

Lesson 8

cultivate learning

Even as infants, our children bang objects together, rub them and even bite them. They simply love experimenting with anything that comes their way and that's really fun to witness. It also reminds us, as adults, to remain curious about our world and how to keep exploring and creatively piece it together.

Creativity is truly sparked by encouraging your baby's sense of curiosity with real objects versus just handing him or her a device to passively watch. For example, I remember when Kathryn was six months old. We handed her a spoon, and she got such a kick out of it. She looked at herself in it on one side and then the other. She banged it on the table, and then we also showed her how to use it - which was fascinating to her! It was a combination of learning and entertainment for all of us.

By participating in your baby's eagerness to learn, you encourage a life-long love for learning to flourish. We want to exemplify how it's essential to always make time to learn and evolve as individuals. Education is not something to just make it through and then be done with; instead we need to promote a culture of continual learning.

In order for us to grow in a positive direction, God desires continual learning for all of us. He wants us to forever develop our relationship with Him, each other, our world, and ourselves. He created our minds to be used as positive powerful tools to build vibrant communities. My daughters would definitely say a phrase I often use is, "Life stays interesting when we keep learning."

Our infants' innate desire to learn is an example of how God created us with a need to keep learning. Let's always keep learning to make a productive and positive impact on our children, each other and the world around us.

The heart of the discerning acquires knowledge,
for the ears of the wise seek it out.
Proverbs 18:15 (NIV)

Lesson 9

everyone is a miracle

When we become a mom, it's inevitable that at some point we look at our baby and think, *Isn't he or she a miracle?* And each baby truly is, but then how come we don't continue to look at each other as miracles once we are grown up? Most of the time, it's because we are in too much of a hurry to really recognize the person at the grocery store or even a work colleague as a miracle. Yet in reality, we are all just grown-up miracles!

At the end of the day, we have all been given various talents that we need to take the time to acknowledge and affirm in each other. Think about how much kinder our world would be if we focused on the good in each person. We may only meet someone for a few minutes out of a lifetime, so to the best of our ability, let's make it a positive few minutes. Let's keep our judgment or criticism quiet and accept others for who they are in that moment. Don't we all want to feel a sense of acceptance? Even if we are watching someone pitch a fit, haven't we at some point lost our cool? Even if someone just cut us off while driving, haven't we at some point done the same thing to someone else?

Come on. Admit it. Giving others the benefit of the doubt and focusing on the good will make for a kinder more patient world. After all, we'd all appreciate being more readily accepted and welcomed for who we are, right? Let's encourage each other to reach our highest potential by taking on the perspective that everyone as a miracle - no matter what their age.

> *You formed my inmost being; you knit me in my*
> *mother's womb. I praise you, so wonderfully*
> *you made me; wonderful are your works!*
> Psalm 140:13–14 (NIV)

Lesson 10

setting priorities

How would you respond if someone asked you what was most important to you in life? Most of us would say, "Our families." Right?

When my first daughter was born, I thought I would pretty much be able to do everything I used to do. I'd just do it all when she slept. However, that notion was quickly proven false. Because the majority of the time, especially while she was still feeding at crazy hours during the night, when she slept, I also slept.

We all have our to-do lists, but what never shows up on any of our lists is what we spend most of our days actually doing as a mother of a newborn: taking care of, cleaning, making food for, feeding, changing, playing with, teaching, and loving our baby. And despite not being written down on any list, our baby is now our top priority.

I remember when someone would ask me, "What did you do today?"

At first, my responses were scattered, and I floundered, which probably gave the impression that I barely did anything. However, over time, I began to respond, "I took care of our baby."

With newborns especially, our priority is "keeping tiny humans alive," as my bracelet reads that my youngest daughter gave me one Mother's Day. We are raising the next generation, and that definitely takes priority over most other stuff - or again as I call it *life maintenance*. After all, moms are essential in order for society to exist - let alone thrive.

Being a mother requires us to really step back and prioritize.

Sometimes I hear people say, "Well, at least all the laundry is done."

Really? All the laundry is done? That is totally a false statement - the laundry is never done. We need to put some life maintenance aside at times and prioritize our children. Trust me. The laundry will not disappear, but someday your baby will have school and a social life of his or her own. And while our goal is to raise independent healthy adults, we also want to build a strong foundation for them and sharing the gift of time with them is part of that.

I remember one Saturday after our second daughter was born, and it was her first time in our pool. My husband and three-year-old daughter were in the pool laughing with her, but instead of staying outside with them, I ran back inside to "finish" the laundry. That was my mindset. I thoughtlessly ended up sorting all the clothes, putting in another load, and then folding the original load I had gone in to complete. Well, forty-five minutes later, my family was getting out of the pool because the girls were tired and ready for naps. I had missed the whole experience! Why? Because I was folding laundry - which we all know wasn't going anywhere! What a missed opportunity! If I had thought about my timing and priorities, I could've easily done the laundry once the girls were napping.

After that, if I caught myself slipping into one of those "must do now" mindsets or mindlessly caught up in another chore, I learned to step back and think about my timing and whenever possible prioritize my family. Then everything else can be factored in.

Especially with a newborn, we may on some days have time and energy for errands, work, and, yes, even laundry, yet on other days we may just get it together enough to take care of our baby. And really that is what's most important. Also, be sure to prioritize being kind to yourself as you transition into your new role as Mom.

Through this lesson, God stresses that our relationships are the priority. Ironically, this distracting and demanding world leaves most of us trying to etch out time to be with our loved ones, our God, and ourselves, but our relationships need to come first. I've learned that when I prioritize prayer each morning, then God helps me more calmly move through the rest of my day. Once we recognize that time with Him is a priority, then everything else falls into place.

God's Ten Commandments are all based on building loving relationships. By mindfully prioritizing God and our loved ones, we remember how come we are doing all the other life maintenance.

When we have this sense of perspective that God comes first, it helps us also prioritize our families and our own well-being. Being mentally and spiritually aware of this order enables us to stay calmer because we know that our priority is to build loving relationships.

There is a time for everything, and a season
for every activity under the heavens.
Ecclesiastes 3:1 (NIV)

Lesson 11

make time to rest

After all the books I read about caring for babies, the one thing that was repeated most often was the importance of them getting enough sleep. In reality, we all feel better when we get enough rest, and not only do we feel better, we respond more patiently and live more joyfully. Studies prove getting enough sleep also keeps us healthier. So in many ways, infants have it right. They sleep a full night and even take naps. Sounds good to me!

My Mimi used to take a nap every day and my mother-in-law, despite how busy she is, also naps daily. Most days I work in a few minutes to at least rest. For example, as I wait in the school pickup line, I plan to at least quietly rest and sometimes even catch a few minutes of actual sleep. It helps me recharge. We don't all require the same amount of sleep, but it is important that we each yield to our individual needs. Unfortunately in many ways our society discourages our need for sleep. Thankfully recent studies showing the benefits of sleep are gaining more publicity.

I often say to my girls as they snuggle in to sleep, this is your time to rest and re-energize your whole being - mind, body and spirit. I encourage them to envision themselves resting in the palm of God's hand. We all need rest and to know someone is holding us can help us feel even more relaxed. Just visualize a mother holding her sleeping baby - what a precious sight.

Let's remember that when we are well-rested, we are more patient and even kinder to ourselves and each other. Rest is a necessary building block for more peaceful and joyful life. So let's make time for it every day and by doing so, we will actually feel more energized.

Come to me, all you who are weary and burdened, and I will give you rest. Take my yoke upon you and learn from me, for I am gentle and humble in heart, and you will find rest for your souls. For my yoke is easy and my burden is light.
Matthew 11:28–30 (NIV)

Lesson 12

be present

A couple of my friends and I were having a conversation one morning about how important it is to focus on the present moment versus getting stuck in the past or worrying about the future. In the midst of us chatting, my daughter was very busy placing her toys in a bucket and then taking them out and putting them in again and taking them out again. All the while, she was getting such a kick out of the process. She was laughing and fully enjoying herself. When we looked at her, I quickly realized, *Wow, she's fully in the present moment.* She didn't even comprehend the concept of time; therefore, she was naturally able to be completely engaged in the moment. What a beautiful gift to truly be in the moment.

God didn't create our sense of structured time. Human beings created it. Of course, we need to abide by it so we live orderly within our society, but how about we change our attitude towards time. Once we realize we can control how our minds think about time, then we empower ourselves to consciously practice being in the present moment. Consequently, when we are living in the moment, we are much more peaceful.

Each day is a little life in and of itself, so we are gifted the opportunity to begin anew each day. Learning from our past is an important part of life, but ruminating in it, doesn't serve us well. Also, we have goals and plans for the future, but worrying about them is a waste of time. Instead proactively planning is needed to get us to where we need or want to be. I often say to my girls, "Focus on now. Look for the good in the now." Being present in the moment, allows us to stay the course in a more calm manner...and even have more fun, too.

Our babies remind us to live this lesson daily - so allow yourself to truly attend to this current stage of life with your newborn. Let's cherish *this* stage because, before we know it, our infants will be asking for the car keys!

This is the day the LORD has made.
We will rejoice and be glad in it.
Psalm 118:24 (NLT)

So don't worry about tomorrow, for tomorrow will bring
its own worries. Today's troubles is enough for today.
Matthew 6:34 (NLT)

Lesson 13

patience & laughter are choices

It's helpful to remember that because babies aren't born with the ability to care for themselves; we need to be patient with the fact that they are *completely* dependent on us. They do not understand how their bodies work or how to clearly communicate and they certainly aren't trying to upset us. As a result, cultivating patience is essential as we develop this new relationship. It's helpful to remember that it's a learning process for *all* of us.

When our babies come into this world, a new relationship begins for all of us. As in any new relationship, it takes time to get to know each other. Therefore, when I would be up during the night, I used to pray for all of us who were awake around the world - I'd pray for all of us to be patient and peaceful with this newly forming bond.

Also, I remember a very early morning when all within a few minutes, I changed a dirty diaper, my baby spit up on me, I spilled my tea, the bottle fell, and I tripped, all while I was trying to figure out why she was crying. In that moment, my husband walked in. Right then and there, we both had a choice to either express complete frustration or laugh. Thankfully, we chose to laugh.

The lesson is that we all need to be patient with this journey and even laugh at ourselves because inevitably, as mothers, we find ourselves in some very unpredictable rather ridiculous situations. After all, motherhood can't really be explained until we are elbow deep in diapers. Rather it's something that needs to be experienced to truly be understood. So welcome!

Our God is patient with us. Imagine how He needs patience as we continually mess up! In turn, He created us with the ability to be patient. And hey, let's face it - on some days it's easier than on others! We're always learning. So let's be patient with our babies, each other, and ourselves as well as choose to laugh in the midst of our challenges as a mom.

As a bonus, when we laugh, we also encourage a sense of humor to flourish in our children, which is extremely valuable (and I'd even say needed) in our crazy world! They watch *every* move we make, so let's help them develop a sense of humor. Also it's simply more fun to laugh with them at times than to always be upset or too serious.

How encouraging it is to know that God designed us to laugh. When we practice patience, we end up also allowing ourselves to laugh more often and that makes life much more enjoyable.

Our mouths were filled with laughter, our tongues
with songs of joy. Then it was said among the nations,
"The Lord has done great things for them."
Psalm 126:2 (NIV)

Be completely humble and gentle; be patient,
bearing with one another in love.
Ephesians 4:2 (NIV)

Lesson 14

life through childlike eyes

Another lesson that God reminds us of, through our infants, is to greet each day with childlike eyes. Our babies greet each day with a natural sense of excitement. They have no expectations—for better or for worse—of what will happen. They simply wake up ready for whatever is to come and are enthusiastic about everyday happenings. Their faces become aglow over people, animals, objects, and even voices that, as adults, we may become desensitized to noticing. If we take note, our children enable us see our world anew every day. Their sense of awe reminds us of how, when we also continue to look at life with fresh eyes, we will find inspiration and reason to stay enthusiastic no matter how old we are.

Consequently, we need to ask ourselves: how are we greeting each day? Hopefully we wake up with a similar sense of enthusiasm as our babies. Despite the barrage of negativity our world spews at us, we need to remain hopeful and focus on the goodness and beauty. Since we are God's children, it's helpful to remember that he created us to with a natural sense of awe that we witness in our children.

I can still visualize how my daughter's eyes lit up when we'd place her on our bed each morning. It was as though we had just landed on a cozy cloud. Each time she just gleamed a big smile; she never took it for granted - she kept noticing it like it was the first time. Or when we'd go for a walk and she'd see a dog, she'd wave and giggle with pure joy again as if it were the first time she saw a dog! Or how she'd close her eyes, smile a bit and lift her face each time she felt a sprinkle of rain start! In this way, our children inspire us to keep this sense of awe.

Our children's enthusiasm for each new day is contagious - if we allow it to be - imagine if we all kept our ability to look at the world with childlike eyes how much more alive our world would be. By continually sending us babies, God reminds us that being childlike in spirit is a positive attribute. Thank you, God, for offering us this inspiration through our infants. Let's be open and look at life with wonder through childlike eyes.

Hear this, you foolish and senseless people, who have eyes but do not see, who have ears but do not hear.
Jeremiah 5:21 (NIV)

Lesson 15

remember the light

When I was pregnant, a friend cautioned me by saying, "While having a baby is amazing, just know that those first few months will be challenging in ways you've never experienced." Therefore, it's important we recognize that while there's much joy with the birth of our baby, often there's also a new level of demand and definitely an adjustment period. Knowing to expect that was very helpful, and I am still thankful that she shared her insight with me because instead of feeling unqualified - or insane - I felt normal when I found it challenging to be a mom. Becoming a mother transforms you in all ways - mind, body and spirit. (Thankfully it's mostly all for the better, I think!)

Since transitioning into motherhood, I've realized that embracing a constant sense of adjustment is key in understanding and making peace with our role as Mom; but there is also a reassuring sense of light at each stage, too. Motherhood is a challenge for all of us at varying levels; however, when we notice the light of God each day either in our babies, within us or those we love or in the world around us, it creates a sense of serenity. Our newborns remind of us to look for the light because they offer us a light we've never experienced. As Mom, we need to notice and value this light as well as continue to encourage our infant's light to shine.

Just as we witness how our infants shine their inner light, we are reminded to shine ours as well. As we deepen our faith, we are encouraged to courageously share our light. As we help our children through various life challenges and make our way through our own, God reminds us that there is always light. We just need to remember to look for it. Let's keep our infants' innate light shining, bravely share ours and encourage others to also shine - in turn we can light up the world one person at a time.

> *"You are the light of the world. A town built on a hill cannot be hidden. Neither do people light a lamp and put it under a bowl. Instead they put it on its stand, and it gives light to everyone in the house."*
> Matthew 5:14-15 (NASB)

Lesson 16

love is what matters most

As a new mother, it's super easy to feel overwhelmed because, as I just mentioned, we are adjusting mentally, physically, and spiritually to our new role as Mom. Not only are we perplexed at times about how to handle our baby, but also we are often tired because of a broken night's sleep and exhausted because of this literally "in our lap" huge responsibility of raising another person! There is so much happening on so many levels.

At moments, I felt like, "Who am I to be raising another person? After all, I'm still trying to figure it out myself!" And we also realize that now that we are mothers - we are mothers forever. Our life as we knew it has been drastically altered, and as a result feeling out of control is understandable. And all those baby books about how to do this or that can be helpful, but they can also at times make you feel worse because none of their recommendations work for you and your child.

I was having one of these moments when my mom slowed me down by simply and yet firmly saying,

"Amy, it's okay. You're doing your best. The most important thing you can do is love your baby. She feels your love." And that's it in a nutshell: love.

God keeps sending us babies to remind us how important love is in our world and that it is only through love that peace will reign. So we need to love each other even in moments of feeling in over our heads. Make a mindful effort to stop whatever activity you are in the midst of doing, especially if you are feeling overwhelmed, and simply pause and love your baby. In fact, thoughtfully love whoever you are with in the moment—your partner, sibling, parent, friend, and so on.

By sending us our own children, God allows us to experience the joy of motherly love. By experiencing this love for our child, God reminds us of how much we are loved as His children. That is the most important reason why babies keep being born, to remind us that we are all children of God and He unconditionally loves us. Our relationship with God is based on love; in turn we need to parent from a place of love.

Imagine all of us raising the next generation from a place of love! Fear wants to overcome our world, but won't be able to if we keep rooting ourselves in love. Our newborns enable us to become aware of a love deeper than we could've ever imagined. Let's share our amazing ability to love not only with our babies, but also with those we meet. God is infinite love and our world needs more love - so let's make a genuine effort to extend love every day.

Therefore, as God's chosen people, holy and dearly loved, clothe yourselves with compassion, kindness, humility, gentleness and patience. Bear with each other and forgive one another if any of you has a grievance against someone. Forgive as the Lord forgave you. And over all these virtues put on love, which binds them all together in perfect unity.
Colossians 3:12–14 (NIV)

Conclusion

Although at their current ages my daughters are more independent than ever, they do still need my help for various reasons. Motherhood is an amazing journey, and it's important to note that, during the years it takes to raise our children, we all learn from and with each other along the way. Hopefully these lessons offered you a new perspective on how to establish a solid foundation upon which to build your mom/child relationship. My hope is that you and your baby grow together in love and become the radiant people you were born to be. I also hope that these lessons strengthen your faith and as a result, enable you to live a more peaceful and joyful life.

Our newborns radiate hope, joy, and love. God also wants each of us to embody these attributes. While our world is riddled with sad and maddening events that can discourage us, our children challenge us to live life more joyfully. God is looking for ways to bless and inspire us every day, and one way He does this is through our newborns. When we take this perspective of also learning from our newborns, we recognize how their presence ultimately encourages love and community. Therefore, it is valuable to realize that they are as much our teachers as we are theirs.

Lastly, I encourage you to journal lessons you learn from your baby. Maybe someday when your child is older you will read them together. I assure you, reflecting on what you recorded is a fun activity to do together!

Enjoy the journey of life together … one day at a time.

I used to believe that prayer changes things, but now I know that prayer changes us and we change things.
St. Teresa of Calcutta

About the Author

Amy M. Collins, M.S.Ed, is a forever-evolving mother of two daughters. She is grateful for her daughters and husband and continues to enjoy being and learning with them.

Amy offers an online course called, "Moms: Courageous Women Raising the Next Generation" which empowers moms to own, clarify and confidently express their role as Mom.

As mothers it's helpful to make time to reflect on this awesome and humbling role we've been given. When we allow ourselves time to process our journey of motherhood, we better recognize the magnitude of our role in raising the next generation. As moms, we need to consciously come together and elevate the valuable role of mothers. Join a class and become part of our universal mothering team.

Please visit www.amymcollins.com for current information.

About the Illustrator

Jessica Wu is a proud mother of a teenage son, Brandon, who keeps her life very busy and well entertained! In addition to her love of being a mother, she is also a professional graphic designer with over 20 years experience working in the greeting card, giftware, tabletop and toy industries. Combining her love of unique characters and graphics, Jessica is currently developing art licensing brands for the entertainment and children's market.

Please visit her website for more information: www.jessicawudesigns.com

Reflections

*my personal infant's
inspirations*

Printed in the United States
By Bookmasters